TO SPEAK

poems

Michelle Elrick

The
Muses'
Company

The Muses' Company Series Editor: Clarise Foster
Cover art by Seth Woodyard
Book design by Relish Design
Author photo by Anna Frenette
Printed and bound in Canada on 100% post-consumer recycled paper.

We acknowledge the financial support of the Manitoba Arts Council, The Canada Council for the Arts and the Government of Canada through the Book Publishing Industry Development Program (BPIDP) for our publishing program.

Library and Archives Canada Cataloguing in Publication

Elrick, Michelle, 1983
    To speak / Michelle Elrick.

Poems.
ISBN 978-1-897289-50-1

I. Title.
PS8609.L58T6 2010   C811'.6   C2010-901725-0

J. Gordon Shillingford Publishing
P.O. Box 86, RPO Corydon Avenue, Winnipeg, MB Canada R3M 3S3

For Kirsten

A coming of age—

Which?

Does it matter?
Pick a number and I will speak my name loudly
that many times.

TABLE OF CONTENTS

ONE

TWO

THREE

FOUR

FIVE

ONE

Bread & Body

Bread

I grind my grandmother's bones to a powder
add a little water from the blue glacier
spit and stir, knead in dry leaves
the yellow fat from new cream
blood of the Northern Pike and sand
carried down to the valley from the mountain.

The dough is stiff. Hidden lumps
break at my touch into splays of dust—
scents of cedar, rain on hot pavement,
curling smoke from a Drum cigarette,
the habits of black flies, Orion's
bow—a consistency of awe and recollection.

In the hour it takes for the bread to rise
glaciers retreat and leave behind
skirts of rubble, a swamp of bones,
old trees fallen, turned to coal.
Mountains are split by the brush of the river,
bridges hang webbed across the water.

I shape the loaf with a roll and even pressure
of hands accustomed to morning prayer.
Score the taut skin with the edge of a knife—
North and South, the passing flights
of birds. Coiled shells of fossils imbedded
inside sleep uninterrupted.

The bread bakes on a board in the sun,
stout, flecked with salt and cheeks burned.
Sweat glistens like dew on my skin
and is taken up on a circling wind.
I break the crust and eat, exhale—
every breath I lose I breath again,

Swinging: Sets

(one)

Someone told me I could go
all the way around the bar
like water in a bucket.
     Race you—
Pumping legs against
the hanging stillness, calling
     Under duck!
we point our feet as high as
     higher!
To the top
of the red and white pinstriped set.
Dad had to drive 12 inch spikes
through each leg
to keep it down.

(two)

At the bell we fight the crowd
for a coveted seat, three
black rubber cradles drop
on long arms
and bear us up, our own
towering lookout.
Far below, the others
skid across the ground.

On the way down we lie
stiff as boards

               hair drags on gravel
               birds swim in the blue
           kids dig through earthen sky.

(three)

No one swings on the 11th Avenue alley set but me
late at night when Clark Drive is quiet
and lampposts alone strut through darkness
dropping orange like peacocks
drag their tails.

Somewhere above, the stars are burning suns.
I reach for them, toes pointed,
neck arched to a curve.
I circle the bar like water

The spikes rock loose—the whole set unearths—
and I take off, a body pressed
between the updraft and the fall.

APRIL (ONE)

We filled our skirts
under the Blossoming Cherry
chased eddies

Snatched the loose, velvety nickels
right out of the pockets of wind
stuck rare whole flowers in our hair

And got married over and over
until supper time
when Mom called us in

Our names still fresh
undefined
in our ears

SWALLOW

Am I a colt?
Are you a whip?
Are you a sack of oats?
Am I a stone?
Are you a mountain?
Are you a miner?
Am I a tennis ball?
Are you a game?
Are you a backhand?
Am I a fire?
Are you a pit?
Are you a matchstick?
Am I a statue?
Are you a kiln?
Are you a can of Krylon?
Am I a dozen eggs?
Are you a hen?
Are you a skillet?
Am I a drink?
Are you a paper umbrella?
Are you thirsty?
Am I a crayon?
Are you a child?
Are you a solarium?
Am I a swallow?
Are you a swallow?
Are we a pack of swallows?

THE MIDDLE NUMBERS

On Monday, you put your good shoes on
straightened the knot of your casual tie
packed a suitcase of loose clothing
and walked to James Street to do laundry.

I found you folding straight creases
into warm shirt sleeves, followed you home
upstairs to the bed where you slept,
where tossing turned your hair into licks and tufts.

In the morning we stood facing each other:
a mere difference of organs.
Us, androgynous,
the sum of all the middle numbers
equaled to perplexity.

We cocked our heads and stared
poked to test the thickness of skin.

You unlocked the suitcase, offered folded shirts.
I left the mirror, used your face to apply the mascara.
You put on the black dress, I wore your sport coat.
You crossed your legs, I shifted my cigarette down
toward the gully of the knuckle.

We drank a glass of beer while the leaves snapped
off the trees and all the colour fell into a parade of brown.

The fog rolled over James Street and froze on the window.
There was nothing left to wash.

EVEN

Before you moved in
I tried to entertain an Italian man
with the peanut brown skin
of my bare August belly
and the pale handfuls of my breasts.

He skipped over it all, tugging
at the black lace and cotton left on,
looking for the vault, the inside room,
its deep, red walls.

With you there is no weapon.
It is all skin and round mountains of bone,
pockets of comfort, an even hand.

Mirror

Hello familiar
curve bone
shapely form

I know your skin
thin as silk
easily rent

I've walked you inside
anxious dark
downstairs

I've tasted you
bitter rind
easily bruised

I see you familiar
windows shades
rattling glass

Hello you familiar
touch touch reflected
touch

To Speak

FORM

We were both single
in the habit of giving our bodies to boys
for the price of a few well-aimed admirations.

We drank gin, pressed close to each other
where there was warmth—our blithe bodies
uncovered bit by bit: You became my mirror.
I pressed my hands to the glass: each line
a semblance of my own form.

Apart now, we are a lost reflection:
your belly swollen to a cradle, your breasts
full of milk; mine, empty
as unused glasses high in a cupboard,
dusted a bit from time to time.

We are both single
in the habit of giving our bodies to boys
for the price of simple difference

While our affections settle like silt
in the fertile heart, nourishment
for each and every greeting, however brief.
I tell you I love you as I catch my own reflection.
I tell you I love you in passing.

To Distinguish

The page is blank
and so being it holds all words

Yet the night is exactly
this temperature

A shiver pricks my skin
to bumps

Twilight sinks
in a black pond

The moon looks shy
to the North

The clock ticks
through the window

My face bears
this expression

My lips shape
a question

To write is to distinguish
all you could from all you did say

There are a multitude of absolutes
to mark the page

PHYSICAL AND SITUATIONAL REASONS

My skin is chapped
because I do not drink enough water
and the climate here predisposes chapping.

I have fallen for you
because you are a kind, gentle man
and I have no will to explore other regions of desire.

I slept until mid-morning
because I did not set the alarm clock
and there is much on my mind that is yet unresolved.

My calves are tight
because I just walked an hour in flat shoes
and my muscles are slack from a winter of little use.

I have a weak appetite
because I have not been eating refined sugar
and my confusion prevents me from seeing the simple
    point in living.

My apartment is a mess
because I have not cleaned it
because I do not know which way it should be cleaned.

TEETH

From the next room I can hear you panting,
hear him grunt with the effort
of pushing himself into you.

Yesterday you told me
about the whore with no teeth
who you met for lunch.
Her dark hair and yours, same cut.
From a distance it'd be easy to make the mistake.

We drank tea while you counted
on your fingers: each fuck
another name in the room between us.

He's the *one*, you said. The last one.

The dim light from the red shade
stained your hands, mostly open
with counting.

She gets paid, you said, I have my teeth.

The differences are small as incisors
brief as a pocket full of coins.

PIECES OF VIRGINITY

Take it away from me, this
one, pinched between my fingers
the last pearl of my grandmother's strand:
an inheritance rung in a circle

Around my throat—the elegant virginity
of daughters. I used to feel it hanging
there, against the straight bones
of my collar. Old thread

Breaks easy. Pieces of virginity—
spit, hands, darkened rooms—sunk
to the seabed of my body, each pearl
hidden in the belly of a shell.

I remember all of their names
and the feeling of each hand
sifting through the fine sand
and the pry of a most limited ecstasy.

Take it away from me, this
one, pinched and lackluster,
it's worth a loose penny.
I have no places left of secrecy.

AMBIGUOUS INFANT

She bulged the natural way
sway-backed and taut
walked the same uneven gait
to the birthing room
and lowered herself
onto white sheets.

She bore the child in blood and cream
spent her prize so long cultivated
into the hands of those waiting
while she waited
in her new emptiness
for a place to put the name.

But there were no testicles for Adam
no vaginal opening for Eve
and the mother, she was just a child—
only now sixteen—
with an ending in her arms
with the suck at her breast.

METROPOLITAIN

Lost on the Paris metro,
company changes quick enough
to keep it always strange.
Graffiti flashes past the window
lit by the train's bright belly
for an instant and a blur—
I forget names immediately,
even my own.
Across the foot place
our knees interlock without touching
though I know your touch,
your knee, your name. It is my own
I have forgotten. Hello.
How are you. I am.
Another introduction
forces the pronunciation out
of the deep warren inside
where precious things are hid in a panic
when the fox is near.
Stop. The company changes.
I stare at the window.
You are the only one I recognize.
My line of sight is bent
by the window's reflection
and taunted by rushes of paint. If only
I could grab a letter, another, patch
gaps in the spelling, form the name
in my mouth. Hello. How are you. I am.
And hear it again. And hear it
again.

TWO

fluttering, a moth

THE LEAK IN THE ROOF
OF THE MONASTERY CHAPEL

The rains came today
taking place of the snow
and the drip
and the drip through the leak
to the floor by the font
I touch holy water to my head
and it slips
to catch in the hair above my eye
(and the drip
and the drip from the faucet
to the tub where I bathed
my body in and out
bent knees and arms held drops
till they dried)
and the drip
and the drip on my head
bowed low as the Abbot
wails old water through the air
and over the rail and
I cannot feel it
caught in my hair
but know it is done

Cocoon

The night weaves
a cocoon

Lulled by the sway
of transformation

Branches creak, bark
against hard bark

This new, fluttering
like a moth inside me

MOUNTAINS AND THE PRAIRIE

Behind me now, the mountains
fade into mottled dusk;

Foothills rock and sway, a mother
with her restless child.

I am crawling onto this flat sheet in darkness
to lie on my back and watch the night

Spark with small guides
and turn round into day.

My body's humps and crevasses
exposed as new minor mountains

Lost on the prairie
and casting brief shade.

TELL THE KING

I am Manitoba,
stretching earth until it loses consistency,
becomes space.

A ragged line of trees
stitches open to empty
in the distance—that edge I fell

from (the lines of your shape)
that (bend of your frame,
taut skin, smooth) assurance.

Here the sky is falling (is falling)
weaving under and above
a blanket without texture.

Only a thin handful of dirt
keeps me from dropping
into this breath of possibility.

There is a rough green line.
There is a body and an open mind
(pieces of it have chosen new

and distinct spheres of orbit).
I am Manitoba: the business of questions:
de-spooling thread unwinding cotton

un fibre un
stitch (stripped)
without form

I know the distance (the paces) between
where I am and where I left you
(the blistered feet of my withdrawal).

Bury me here (under this handful of dirt).
Send a cloud to mark my grave
and the wind to bear my spirit around

and around this drifting orb.
That distant line of trees will be my legacy:
A place to measure

how far away we come
from what we love
in search of something better.

Routes 1, 17, 403

From the mountains, the line dips into Banff
and rolls: Bowness, Brooks, the bowl of Medicine Hat—

I'm changing my name, she says.

a gathering wave up Swift Current, Moose Jaw
the crest of Regina, Indian Head

How come? he says. But really, does it matter?
I always call you Baby.

and sinks again
into Wolseley, Grenfell, Broadview.

Well, I've got to leave something behind.

It settles a moment, Virden, Brandon
then a stretch between the long lakes

You left plenty.

and Winnipeg, St. Boniface.

Not something then, someone.

It turns at Dryden, then Ignace,
to a ditch at Fort William, Port Arthur and climbs

What's it gonna be? he says.

around the broad chest of Lake Superior.
It pulls apart at Marathon,
reunites at the twins: Wawa and Michipicoten.

You & me. Larry. Lori...

Down the slope to Sault Ste. Marie, then Echo Bay,
Blind River, Sudbury and south.

It's got a fairy tale ring, she says, an Adam & Eve.

A drop into Parry Sound, the crossroad at Orillia.

Baby, I guess that makes you my rib.

It fractures into Toronto,
breaks into a star.

BASIC MATERIALS

"We are entering into the night in which he is present
without any image, invisible, inscrutable, and beyond any
satisfactory mental representation." —Thomas Merton

What does one do in the dark but grope—
glancing fingers along the mortar and brick
leaving bits of skin and blood behind.

What is left but substance:
the foot, the other foot
the vapour of breath and mouth full of tongue.

What more than shapes
one can discern from a symbol,
running over the angles and meeting lines.

What is there to do but reach
for a hand to replace the hand before
and finding none, begin again

With the basic materials, this business of knowing.
A new hand whittled by the craft of one's own,
a hand-fashioned hand to fill up the palm.

Epigraph

Maybe there is a way
when I cannot find faith
for it to find me
snatch me up
in a lover's embrace—

heart palpitating
a rose in my cheeks.

THE ORGAN

Blue speakers flank the nativity
struggle to fade into the wall:
shocking lumps of box and mesh
and a wire, straight as a drip leading down.

It all happened in the seventies, she says,
as she flicks the switch and the thing blinks on.
Everyone was doing it, the meticulous dismantle,
carting up the bellows.

She touches a key with the soft tip of her finger
the reproduction belches like a brash ghost
haunting the empty few pipes left
ornamental on the wall behind the tenors.

In a photograph, 1912,
we find the full pipes in sepia tones
fixed and straight as my best posture
their open throats ready.

Closing Prayers

*The primary word I-Thou can be spoken only with the
whole being. Concentration and fusion into the whole being
can never take place through my agency, nor can it ever take
place without me. I become through my relation to the Thou;
as I become I, I say Thou.*
    All real living is meeting. —Martin Buber

I am leaving the church.
In the quiet, everyone else has their heads bowed.

In ancient China women bound their feet
to keep them from growing.

Outside, Elm trees sway,
limber with new sap

River ice breaks into a jamboree
of rafts, slow jostling

A pigeon decomposes in the snow,
flecks of iridescence in the new mud

My lungs make brief clouds
in the air around my face.

I can walk long and far
until the steeple disappears

Breathe prayers
with no body to say them to.

Listen for the resonance
of the pitch of my voice

That whom it vibrates against,
that Thou which I am thanks entire.

THREE

In it. Being.

ON BEING

Approximate the temperature of sun on your bare skin
not with a number in rising degrees
but with a recollection of the sun's heat,
another moment spent in it.

In Your Home

Cooling pipes box fan creak
of the basement door
appliance hums the night
cats computer tower North wind
moth wings on glass television
music your mother's cigarette
lighter clothes falling
footsteps shower your hands
through your beard dogs
pant distant fog horn
coyote gulls a bottle
cap drops your sister blow-drying
car starts breathing sigh
blood in your heart the words
that never leave
my mouth

LOOKING DOWN, OVERHEARING

Long sirens pull up the mountain
on currents of hot air: fire engine
weaves the idling stream of cars
on route to panic.

In its wake, traffic resumes.
Displaced sound washes uphill,
unconcerned as driftwood
gently knocks against the shore.

Wind chimes, engines accelerate,
new, stiff leaves crash
in small sound around/between
an ambulance, now, another.

April (two)

April gathers her dress
in hand for a dance.

Boughs full of flowers even before
the first leaves, every hair

Pinned up, nails filed. Dandelions
(who know nothing of death)

Stand small and yellow
unfolding their crowns.

Notes spin up quick music, her weight
is all in her toes. The storm

Has roots in all directions,
short sleeves show off her goose flesh.

New puddles already drain
in the beds. She's got a wild look

Under that red cherry smile
for the stiff ones who ask her,

Pale and winter-killed.
Her answer is always yes.

ON GARDENING INSTEAD OF SMOKING

In the garden your hands
burrow deep as tulip roots
timid as their forays from the bulb

And as roots draw in rain
you also draw, bathe pale jointed fingers
in humus and clay

Allow soil to make new
demands of you, to force itself
under your nails

Into the cracks of skin—
you submit to the absurdity
of this wash. It is cool.

The worm touches your ring
finger with its blind head.
Wait

For the silk of its body to pass by
though the moment is long
and the dew soaks your trousers.

Alongside the abandoned fruit peels
and mouldering leaves
you let yourself be changed

Into a healthy bed of rot and seed
while the tulips, in small measures,
unfold.

Michelle Elrick   42

BLUE LIGHT, YELLOW LIGHT

Evening blue swells
until dusk is ink monochrome

I flick on the light:
colours bloom in the spill

Yellow sparks the water glass
 illumines the stamen of the flowering cactus

Blue meets Yellow
at the window

They make a line of their distinct sensibilities,
stare with infinite patience at the difference

Yellow is a bead of sap
moving up the bone of a pine

Blue is a duck gone under the pond
with no direction in mind

256 PAPER MACHINE

Machine work packs hours into cartons
a dozen at a time, six to six
sometimes sunrise looks a lot like sunset,
the hour on the punch clock no help.

The windows meant to remind us
which shift is day, which shift is night
by the colour of light they show,
blue or butter yellow.

We take our turns at the window, staring
at the cottonwood grove across the river
noting the casual sway and flicker of leaves
when the wind combs through.

After sunset, night is heady perfume
I press my face against the screen
listen under the factory roar and clatter
for frogs.

The thin wire gives a little
against the weight of my face, nose and lips
make marks in the dust, touch
the white moths on the other side.

BULRUSHES

Even the city is made of open space
busy with wind, the shuffle of seeds.

Take it apart and look—
a tree, a field, a lump of sod
a hill, a flock, a piece of sand—

We are all bulrushes,
cattails and moss
drinking from roots
wet in thaw.

FOUR

a word with no echo

To Speak

[Saturday]

Three words, shaped on the tongue and placed in air
if well-weighted will hang there
like a balloon
made of canvas that won't tear.
I can watch them.

Yesterday, as we said good-bye, your coffee stood
on the roof of the car, only briefly tasted
and I thought about the disappointment that follows
forgetting something so nearly full.

You entered Fargo airport with your hands full of things.
I looked back once, only for a moment,
turned the key in the ignition
and began to portion out distance, back to Canada
with the emptiness of the other seats
and the words in my head, ringing
unspoken.

In your absence, I only remember
a brief assortment of things: the lilt of your voice in a question,
the expression on your face when you're reading,
the way you stretch your neck when you're tired.
Not even all of these together make up
what it is to be with you.

I boarded the bus this morning, back to the coast,
though I have tried to speak, a sigh is all that ever comes.

Outside, the sky is alive like it was in North Dakota: rain sheets
and spreads of sunlight, towering
black-bottom clouds.
I haven't seen any kale since we left the field that morning,
our bellies full of green.
Here it is canola reaching for the horizon
like a luminescent yellow sea.

I wonder how far. I wonder the paces between us
and the height of the waves in the deep Pacific.
I wonder at my thoughts. Whether
they will pitter out on their own,
or be stuffed away,
or forced to multiply unnaturally
under catalytic dreams.
I know the taste of longing like a sweet poison on the tongue
and the addiction to vacancy.

The late afternoon sun has come out and brightened
this field of Saskatchewan. Just as soon it is gone.
Just as soon, just as soon, just as long.

Across the aisle, a woman cuts a peach in two halves
and gives one to her dark-haired companion.
Later, she passes him the carton of rice milk and he drinks;
she slips a half-piece of dark chocolate between his lips
and he wraps it in his mouth.

My silence seems inevitable
as if I cannot afford to give anything away.
As if I have given it all already, given it to you.
As if love is an emptying, and in need
of a like-love in return to have fulfillment.

I can see the angle of his acceptant jaw.

[Sunday]

Outside Calgary station, the sun is about to rise.
I calculate the time by the colour of light,
then I calculate the number of suns yet to rise
before hello ties up the ends of our good-bye.
It is immeasurable, it is
equal to the present moment—
dawn brightens my skin,
this city like a Polaroid image
gently shaken from the dark
—my breath and expiration.
The air is crisp with forgetfulness,
a perpetual awakening.

It would be different if you were dead.
Then to forget would be to lose you entirely.
As far as I can see there is no loss here,
only a moment between.

Approaching the mountains, the road begins to twist and coil.
The landscape gathers me in her many folds: gradient, fir trees,
water always cutting stone.

By tonight I will be with my family
who know nothing of you,
nothing of the utter difference of the plains,
yet they know me, define me
as these mountains define my movement.
It is good for me to be here so soon after speaking *I love you*.

To speak *love* the word *I* must be spoken.
To speak *I* is to know myself as both common and specific,
one in relation. This place rises around me like a room of mirrors;
blue-green rock bites at the sky, swallows fractions, a third.

At times I have only whispered *I*
(at times not said it at all)
tried to pour myself into my idea of your desire.

Instead of *I*,
I speak *the one I imagine you desire.*
This is an incredibly lost and worthless thing to say.

Where have you gone?
Even if I speak *I* and also *love*, what good is it
if there is no *you*? Can love even be spoken without *you*?

None of it exists for me now. All that exists is
the plush back of the seat in front of me and the light,
flashing like a strobe on this page
as the sun bursts between trees.
What is any of it, really?
What is the prairie? How broad
does an Elm tree spread? What shade
of green leaf filters the setting sun?
What is the distance between two
neighbouring houses? How small
can a year become? As small as this?
As small as a forgetting?
You were my friend. Us in a box of Winnipeg.

Good-bye is like admitting all the things I will never know.
And the questions, pouring slowly over.

[Monday]

When I opened my eyes she was there, still asleep beside me,
our bodies sharing the duty of warmth under this one blanket.
My sister, twenty-nine months nine days younger,
now a mother of her own.
We are at the usual campground, adults
where we were once children.
The others haven't changed: lake and cedar,
wet fern of the rain shed, wind nearly always from the sea.

Love is less simple to speak than *I* and *you*.
It is a twisted maze though my will is to stay straight.
It bears me up, gives me ground.

If you were here I would show you the patch of moss
which my niece pulled from an old Douglas Fir. It broke free
still attached to a nickel of bark. We ruffled the fronds:
variegated greens and feathered edges catalogued
between our fingers.
Now, it is replaced in a crack of the trunk, wedged deep
with our best wishes.

In case you ever come here it will be waiting for you: a gift.

Love is not a thing to have or a thing to give
but a state of being with others, even all.
It is not a clutch, it is not an own. Love is
regardless. It is an open hand.
A word with no echo.

To speak *love* is complete. Nothing at all is lacking,
nothing missed or forgot.

[Tuesday]

I brought your sleeping bag along. It is much lighter
and more compact than mine, plus I didn't think you'd mind.
Last night you were in my dream as I slept in your scent.
Awake now, I put my head under the cover and breathe,
eyes closed. There you are.

This is not an experience of your presence.
This is only what lingers—a suggestion of the whole.
I sleep in it, conscious of how my own scent stays behind,
mixes in, makes it not just you, but us,
which is a nice thought, but not the truth.

Whoever *you* are, to me you are only what I remember.

It is surprisingly easy to change the past.

I sculpt the statues of memory by hand.
There they stand, caricatured and grotesque,
without breath or justification,
disconnected from their one glorious stage
of subtle interaction, at the mercy of the interpreter.
These hands do their best (all things considered)
but the job is infinitely difficult and the lighting is poor.

I put my head back under the cover.
There you are.
You are made in me.

[Wednesday]

As I sit against a tree in the windy shade of the lake
the bark against my back is rough and painful.
If I look up to the boughs and let my hair fall
it is long enough to muffle the pain.

There is nothing to be said about longing
but that it dissolves the momentary ground I stand on.

In its wake
I am different yet the same,
chilled in the shade yet also warm,
empty yet full, full of sensation
and the image of that white goose feather caught
in the dry grass at my feet.
I want to say hello to *you*
even as I am saying good-bye.
Instead I say merely *hello*.
The cold is becoming too cold.
I am moving back now, into the sun.

FIVE

the slow articulation

GINGER AND LILACS

The scent of ginger and lilacs
spice pricks the lungs
the delicate rot
colouring in
between edges
what is, what is not
the sweet speaks the spice
the edges of skin
my hand cups the tea
there is no more time
to spend here
the lilacs bloom the room smells
of ginger and ticking clocks
the fullness made of you
and I, cloth, light
and sound, the scent
of ginger and lilacs,
the tick,
tock, new, known
(I love) other than edges
beyond hello and losing
between the scent of ginger
this lilac
between me and unending
is you, clocks
and their tocking

To a Friend Leaving for Africa

(one)

Soon you will be full
of distance: the ocean a cup of cold water
emptied into your mouth
the desert a mean grit in your teeth

Waiting,
heavy with your portion,
for the ache of such abundance
to subside

(two)

You are a lily, your long root untied
and trailing behind you and beneath
the flow of a thick river

This dance of draw and floating
this tug of length and weight

All the shores that pass
hold you with open hands

(three)

We are gardeners of statues
our hands are full of clay

And busy with the chisel and the fine gold leaf
fashioning a time into memory

The tap tap and the chink chink
the wet clay changing to the colour of dust

This slow articulation of hello and goodbye
pulled from stone and eroding

AFFECTION

how we fill our empty hands the bricks we hold the aim
at the window the effort of a decent pitch
the place in the belly where the grunt comes
from the pull of the ball from the socket the sound

of a wall of glass falling the thud
of a weight on the area rug the ache that occupies
the shoulder the length of days the tenderness of a torn
muscle the pain of a sudden

gesture how when the draft in the room is full as wind
we bend hold the dustpan the brush
the heap of glinting pieces how

we wonder at the cost of repair

TOPOGRAPHY OF A TYPICAL BIRD

This is how I understand
what we are: compartmentalize:
break the dynamic whole into pieces,
each with its own name: Breast.
Lores. Nape. Tail. (but please)
I beg each not to take its independence,
not to break our graceful flight
into a shower of feathered parts
gaining velocity and sight of detailed ground—
Rump. Thigh. Tarsus. Claw.
names shouted as they fall.
Something so newly born
grown already old
enough to say I.
A million pieces, a chorus
of noise.

SONG FOR YOUNG LOVERS

I want to love you in the idle days of old age
once all this angst has expired
and the meaninglessness of life
is nothing but a broken record, scratching
a weak and comic tune

Rich with dissonance, harmony
and the space between notes
where silence sounds through.

LUNCH, LATE AUTUMN

Last Wednesday at lunch, Opa forgot the bread rolls
and dished the gravy out twice.

He doesn't bother anymore with false teeth or variety
this week, last week, the week before, ham.

In this late season, he is shifting
foot to foot in waiting postures.

His hands have become soft, plump sausages
transparent skin wrung at the window

While the leaves process: canary yellow,
pumpkin pie brown, the odd, tragic green.

The days are getting shorter, he says,
his feet shuffle him between the afternoon rooms

All I want is a good sleep
so when I wake up, this heaviness is gone.

Yet the maples crisp to brittle rosettes
and in the morning the trees are full of sky

Black branches wet with rain
count the time like the hands of his watch.

Everything is quiet but the news.
He listens to the weatherman forecast

Another day before sleeping. *Days are getting shorter*,
he says. It is dark when he turns down the bed.

Michelle Elrick   72

ODE TO A MARCH SUNFLOWER

Look at what the year has done to you:
coaxed your first pale thumb
from wet earth, pulled you tall and hefty
up five sure feet.

You once stared East for the coming sun
mocked its shape and yellow.
Your stalk, once green and proud with water
flaunted broad leaves, waving.

Now you are curled and stiff
brown with mould and spent extravagance
waiting your last few days in silent thaw
with thoughts of your seeds.

BURYING TUNE

There is a tune that goes along
with the burying of the dead

It's the sound of a muggy haze
turning into a thunderhead

Put your ear to the soil
if you cannot hear the notes

Stick your hand in the beehive
and let the honey coat your throat

It is time, take the shovel,
anywhere is fine

And if you cannot sing, just dig instead
make it deep enough and wide

DITCHES

There was a bridge for trains to cross
the deep farm ditches
with a small space for us to sit,
hang our young legs,
flick cigarette butts
into the dark
        wait!
they hiss, extinguish.

You said, *this
is where I come to be. Come
with me. Be
here—
it's best when the train comes past.*
and I agree
because no one should be alone to grieve.

Split, each
down the middle.
Ditches run the lengths of us.

So we sit here, over the darkness,
over the rippling black water
where unsteady stars waver.
We wait for trains.

Smell of creosote, the bridge that
moans and bows under their passing.

It is a good thing
there are ties to hold each crossing
no matter what the weight.

The dead leave ditches
and we are tied
that the heaviness might pass over.

To Speak

GRAVESIDE: HOW TO SAY GOOD-BYE

Unroll the sod
the mound has settled.
Match up the edges
where the spade cut
rectangular hatches
into the earth's bright skin.
Stomp and water.
Nod to the company
at hand: dandelion seeds
the common housefly
the scent of July roses.
The silk lining damp by now
and the body leaking
into the mouths of worms.

Pick the grass and taste
the supple white root.
Graze until she is eaten.
Good-bye learned as slowly
as the body learns to decompose.

April (three)

Above the street, the corridor
of young cherry trees
(still twiggy and un-leafed)

Is shaken empty even now
by the abrupt hand
of South wind.

Gusts flood the gutter
with petals, pink and bruised
to the point of transparency.

On branches, tight knots
of new leaf begin their slow unraveling
like a tongue loosening to speak.

ACKNOWLEDGEMENTS

Earlier versions of the following poems were first published in literary journals. "256 Paper Machine" in *Canadian Literature*, "Swallow" in *Event*, "The Leak in the Roof of the Monastery Chapel" and "On Gardening Instead of Smoking" in *The Fiddlehead*. Thank-you to the editors of these fine publications.

The cover illustration is from the painting "Like a Moth" by Seth Woodyard, done on commission. Special thanks to Seth.

Thanks to Clarise Foster for selecting this book from the many, and for careful editing and guidance.

Thanks also to St. Margaret's Anglican Church and the Manitoba Writer's Guild for studio space while this book was completed.

And to the many friends, strangers and family members who live in these poems, thank-you for the meeting.

WORKS CITED

Buber, Martin and Ronald Gregor Smith, translator. *I and Thou.* London, Continuum, 1937.

Merton, Thomas. *Contemplative Prayer.* New York, Image Books edition, 1971.